Published in the United States in 2013 by @ Raburn Publishing, a division of Stephen Raburn + Associates, LLC

Edited by Melanie Bourgeois

To order this and other Raburn Publishing books visit www.raburnpublishing.com

Oh Dad! is a registered trademark of Raburn Publishing

ISBN-13:
978-1468171556

ISBN-10:
1468171550

FROM THE PUBLISHER:

If I had a quarter for every time I've heard those words!

As an active father of two amazing little girls and admittedly a little on the goofy side, "Oh Dad!" is indeed a frequently spoken phrase in my house... accompanied by obligatory eye-rolling and (usually) uproarious laughter as well. It was the obvious name for a line of books I've been looking to create.

Truth of the matter is that I love every second of being "Dad."

In many ways, I'm typical of a growing subgroup of dads. Generally speaking, fathers today are more active in the everyday care and decision-making of children than those of previous generations. That's partly due to the natural evolution of parenting, I think. And partly due to economics. More dads are able to work from home or have flexible work schedules than in the past. And women are earning more money, so dads aren't necessarily the automatic breadwinner for the family these days. That's the good news. The bad news: there are an awful lot of unemployed dads out there too.

Whatever the reason, there's a bunch of us spending a lot of time with our children. And that's got to be a good thing.

But the publishing biz has been slow to catch on. With most magazines and books "Parenting" is code for "Mom," it seems. In my experience, there's a dearth of resources for dads.

Oh Dad! is a line of books created to fill that void: fodder for those of us who aspire to be greatest dad in the world (but need a little help).

Help is just what foodie Sarah Spigelman offers in Oh Dad's! first book.

Ms. Spigelman is a renowned Manhattan food writer, blogger and connoisseur of edible delights. She wrote "What's for Breakfast, Dad?" for us, which is in equal parts intro to the kitchen and awesome cook book. Sarah gently leads us into the kitchen and shows us that it's not such a scary place after all – once you know a few basic rules and techniques. The recipes? Think bacon candy and waffle-wiches.

"What's for Breakfast, Dad?" is a perfect example of what Oh Dad! is hoping to provide: fun, quirky, insightful, useful books for devoted dads and the eye-rolling kids who love them. Enjoy.

-Stephen Raburn

{MENU}

{INTRODUCTION}

Fire. Knives. The possibility for blood, gore and disease everywhere you turn. No, it's not the torture chamber of some medieval castle. It's...YOUR KITCHEN. But this doesn't have to be your perception of it. Sure there is a lot of danger there, but there is also fun, creativity, and bonding with your kids.

Learn a few simple terms, master a couple of techniques and you can create an environment that is part learning, part fun and entirely delicious!

So you never picked up a spatula in your life and you can't tell your gateau from your ganache? Who cares? Did you know that Julia Child didn't even open her oven until she was over 30 years old? By the time you are done with this handbook, you will be a pro. Or, at least you will be able to fool your kids into thinking you are one.

And no one's fingers will get chopped off in the process.

{TERMS}

Here are the cooking terms that will take you from making microwave quesadillas all the way

to roasting a duck:

Chopping cutting your ingredient into small but not tiny pieces

Dicing cutting your ingredient into tiny, even pieces

Boiling heating a pot of liquid until large bubbles appear and continue to appear quickly and consistently

Steaming boiling a small amount of liquid in a pan, then as it evaporates into steam, cooking your
 ingredient via that steam

Sautéing heating a small amount of fat in a saucepan until a piece of bread sizzles when it is dropped in,
 then reducing the heat and slowly cooking the ingredient until the ingredient turns golden brown
 and the sugars caramelize

Peeling taking all of the skin off a vegetable

Roasting cooking something in the oven on a relatively low and slow heat for a long period of time

{A FEW BASICS}

Now that you have all the terms down, let's go over a few techniques:

Dicing an Onion

This is one of the hardest things to learn and also one of the most useful techniques. Thank you to Adam Roberts, The Amateur Gourmet. With it, you can doctor a jar of spaghetti sauce, make instant mashed potatoes taste homemade, create the scrambled eggs of your dreams...the possibilities are endless. Point is - you have a diced onion, you have a meal. The reason it is important to dice an onion is that it is impossible to quickly cook large pieces of onions. The smaller, more even the cuts, the faster the onion cooks. The faster it cooks, the faster your kids eat.

1} Slice the root and top end off of the onion so that the onion itself is exposed through the skin

2} Make a slice - not all the way through, just through the first layer of the onion - lengthwise over the onion's skin. Remove the skin - if you take off a layer of onion, that is okay too

3} Set the onion on the root or top end, so the onion is flat, and slice through the top of the onion. You should now have two half moons of onions

4} Now turn one of your onion half moons on its flat side so the curved side is facing upwards

5} Starting at the root end (you will know because the root end will have a light brown circle where the root used to be), a tiny bit up from the brown circle, make cuts lengthwise through the onion When you are done, you should have a half moon that has many long cuts, all the way through to the cutting board, but that is still attached at the root end

6} Now you want to slice into the onion the other way - horizontally - from the front towards the back. It's like you are making a little plus sign in the onion. Once again, stop before you hit the root

7} Finally, take your onion and chop downwards, vertically, so that the onion pieces fall away in tiny even squares. Throw the uncut root end away

TA-DA!!! YOU HAVE SUCCESSFULLY CHOPPED AN ONION!
Now we are going to move on to sautéing it.

1) Put a skillet on the stove and turn the heat to medium high – about a 6 if your stove dial turns to 10

2) Pour a bit of olive oil, butter, or nonstick spray in your pan

3) After a few minutes, put one piece of onion in the pan. If it sizzles, throw all of it in. If it doesn't, wait a few more seconds and then add the onions. If you add the onions too early, they will just absorb the oil and get soggy instead of turning sweet and golden

4) After you throw the onions in, turn the heat down to medium low-about a 4. In about 20 minutes, you will have a golden brown substance in the pan that is sweet, salty, full of oniony flavor and ready for any myriad of applications

While the onion cooks is a great time to get your kids involved. Ask them what they want to make with it – do they feel like adding some crushed tomatoes to the skillet and making a homemade pasta sauce? Maybe they have been studying India in school and want to throw some curry powder in there to see if they like it. If you have really adventurous eaters, a tiny dab of cayenne pepper or chipotle hot sauce might awaken their inner chili-head. Or, you can make them the simplest and possibly best meal ever. It's one that the kids can help you make and that they will love to eat: SCRAMBLED EGGS!

INGREDIENTS

4 eggs

1 Sautéed onion (freshly sautéed, still in pan over medium low heat)

2 tsp. Salt

1 tsp. Pepper

1/3 cup Shredded cheese (optional)

1} Break eggs into a large bowl

2} Whisk with a fork until all eggs are yellow and homogenous

3} Add the salt and pepper

4} Pour into onion skillet

5} Turn heat down low – to a 2

6} Stir continuously with fork or spatula so small curds form – this should take no more than 5-7 minutes

   depending on if you like your eggs softer (less cooked) or harder (more cooked)

7} Right before you are done cooking, stir in cheese and mix eggs around until cheese is melted

   and stringy

8} Serve

The kids can break the eggs and add the seasoning. If they are about 8 years old, they can even do the

cooking, with your supervision. Nothing makes kids want to try more foods and experiment with different

tastes than cooking a dish themselves.

And nothing makes dads feel better than being able to cook a delicious meal entirely by themselves.

And now you can.

What else can you do? Well, the truth is almost anything. Your kids can use the microwave, and older kids can even use the stove or knives as long as you are there to supervise. Here are some fun ideas:

1} Come home with 5 ingredients and give the kids half an hour to think of and create a meal, Iron Chef Style

2} Theme meals like: All orange (maple glazed carrots, macaroni and cheese, butternut squash), baby themed (baby back ribs, baby corn salad, baby new potatoes), or themed around their favorite TV show (krabby patties, anyone?)

3} Watch a cooking show together on the weekend then set out to make it that day. Make a day of it by heading to the grocery store or greenmarket then coming home and spending all day in the kitchen.

4} A "Dare "meal" -each of you gets to choose a food that the other has never tried and the other person HAS to try it! This is a great way to get your kids to try beans, spinach, lamb or anything else you want to incorporate into their diets. Just don't be shocked if they want you to try strawberry flavored yogurt or candy so sour it will pucker your lips!

5} Dinner and a movie – watching Lady and The Tramp? Pull out the spaghetti. Harry Potter? Better make some Butterbeer (otherwise known as cream soda and vanilla ice cream served frosty mugs). It's easy enough to make a themed meal with a movie, and if you eat when the people in the movie are eating, your kids will feel more involved and invested than ever!

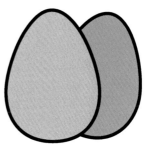

{BREAKFASTS}

The most important meal of the day. One of the most fun meals of the day. Remember that whatever

ingredients you like are what you should use. If your kids are allergic to peanut butter, substitute almond

or cashew butter. If they hate tomatoes, use green salsa. If they like spicy, feel free to toss some hot sauce

in whatever you like. The thing to remember is that these recipes are starting off points. There is no way to

really mess them up - get creative with your favorite add ins and substitutions. Let's go beyond pancakes

and frozen toaster pastries and really explore fun and easy recipes that no one else's dad will be making

this weekend!

ALL RECIPES SERVE 2

BACON CANDY

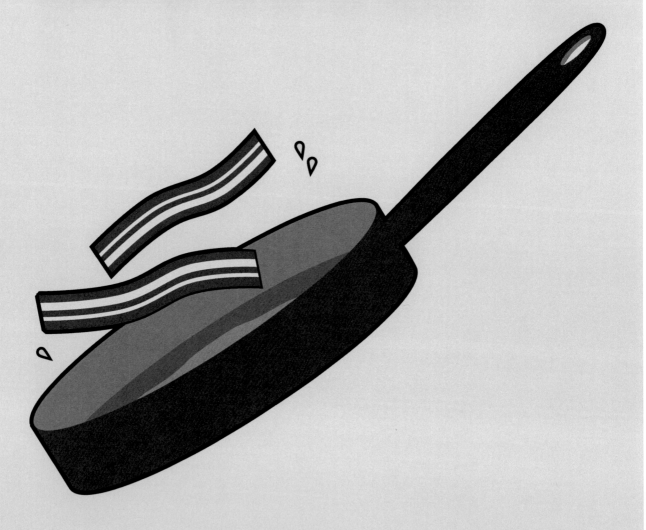

You know how good bacon tastes when you dip it into maple syrup? Imagine that times 10 and that is this recipe. Smokey, savory, intensely sweet, with notes of molasses and even cinnamon in there. It makes French toast taste deeper, BLTs taste fresher and goes just swell with a dab of chipotle-infused ketchup. Kids love how sweet it is and you will love how simple it is to make.

DIRECTIONS

1} Preheat the oven to 350° and tinfoil a baking sheet

2} Lay the bacon out on the sheet in a single layer

3} Sprinkle the brown sugar over the bacon

4} Pack the brown sugar on the bacon in a thick blanket

5} Place in the oven for about 7 minutes, or until the sugar has fully melted (and almost black in some spots), and the bacon is not fully stiff, but there are no translucent spots on the bacon. It will continue to cook after you take it out of the oven, so you don't want it fully crisp yet

6} Wait 5 minutes. You must wait. You can NOT eat this until it has cooled. Otherwise it will burn your mouth and the flavor will not be fully infused into the bacon. When the bacon has stiffened, it is ready to eat

INGREDIENTS

1 Pack of Bacon

1/2 Box of Brown Sugar

NOTES:

FRIED
PB&B

Nothing beats a spoonful of creamy peanut butter...unless, of course, it's peanut butter mixed with sweet bananas and nutmeg.

DIRECTIONS

1} Spread the peanut butter over two slices of the toast

2} Place bananas and any other mix ins on peanut buttered bread

3} Heat the butter in the pan over medium low heat (3 out of 10) until the butter melts

4} Place the peanut buttered bread, peanut butter side up, in the pan. Be careful, it may splatter

5} Put the plain piece of bread on top of the bread in the pan, making a sandwich

6} In about 2 minutes, or when the toast is lightly golden, carefully flip it

7} In about 2 minutes, or when the other piece of bread is golden and toasted, take the bread out

8} Top with powdered sugar and jelly and serve

INGREDIENTS

4 Slices Sandwich Bread
(whatever you have in the house)

1/3 Cup Peanut Butter
(creamy or crunchy, room temperature)

1 Banana
(sliced into small coins)

1 tsp. Nutmeg

1 Tbls. Butter
(room temperature)

Powdered Sugar, Jelly or Jam to garnish

Optional: Raisins, slices of candied bacon, peanuts, any other add ins you may like

NOTES:

TOAD IN THE HOLE

These are known as egg in bread, but it's so much more fun to call it toad in the hole! It's shocking how fun plain old eggs and toast become when your kids can cut the hole in the bread themselves and see how the egg forms to the bread. Serve it with candied bacon, microwaved turkey sausage or a fruit salad for a wholesome breakfast. Use multigrain bread for the most nutritional value, raisin walnut bread for a sweet and savory combination or sourdough bread for the tangiest, tastiest toad in the hole ever created.

DIRECTIONS

} Cut a hole out of your bread with the rim of a drinking glass

2} Melt the butter in a skillet over medium heat (4 or 5 out of 10)

3} When the bread has turned golden on one side, flip it

4} Place the peanut buttered bread, peanut butter side up, in the pan. Be careful, it may splatter

5} Crack the eggs directly into the center of the hole of the bread. If you need to, crack it into a bowl, then tip the bowl into the center of the hole. The point is to deliver the egg into the middle of the hole without mixing or scrambling it – the goal here is sunny side up, not scrambled

6} Cover the pan so the egg cooks to your exact preference

7} Slide the bread and egg out of the pan with a spatula, taking care not to puncture the yolks

8} Season with salt and pepper and serve

INGREDIENTS

2 Eggs

2 Slices of bread

2 Tbs. butter

Salt and pepper to taste

NOTES:

TROPICAL FRUIT OATMEAL

With a packet of oatmeal, some half and half and a can of pineapple in the house, you can make a warming, stick-to-your-ribs breakfast that will remind you of summer even in a snowstorm. If the day is really dark and dismal, turn your Pandora to a Hawaiian station, rent Blue Hawaii on Netflix and turn the day into a breakfast luau! This is a great chance to introduce your kids to tropical flavors you love. If you want to put lychees or coconut flakes in there, go for it!

DIRECTIONS

} Prepare the oatmeal as according to instructions, replacing the water in the recipe with your half and half

2} Drain the fruit cocktail and place the fruit in oatmeal

3} Add the coconut and vanilla extract, if desired

4} Serve

INGREDIENTS

2 Packets instant oatmeal
(plain or cinnamon flavor)

1 small can tropical fruit cocktail or other canned tropical fruit
(i.e. litchi, pineapple, etc)

Enough half and half or cream to replace the water in your oatmeal recipe

1/2 cup Flaked sweetened coconut

1 tsp. vanilla extract
(optional)

NOTES:

FAST FOOD EGG SANDWICHES

Whoever says they don't crave a fast food sandwich every once in a while is a dirty rotten liar – don't trust them! This recipe will fulfill all of your fast food cravings and, as a bonus, you can enjoy it while watching cartoons with your kids instead of yelling at all the bad drivers on the road.

DIRECTIONS

1} Scramble the eggs, salt and pepper in a small, greased microwaveable bowl

2} Microwave the eggs with the bowl of water in the microwave for 1 minute at a time, stirring after each minute, until eggs are firm

3} Microwave Canadian bacon for 20 seconds, or until warm

4} Put one slice each of cheese (or divide the grated cheese evenly) each on 1 half of each English muffin, and microwave for 30 seconds at a time or until the cheese is melted

5} Layer the egg, bacon , onions and ketchup on top of the cheesy English muffin

6} Put the other half of the English muffin on top and serve

INGREDIENTS

2 English muffins, toasted

2 slices Canadian bacon

2 eggs

1tsp. each salt and pepper

2 slices cheese or 1/4 cup grated cheese

2 Tbls. Ketchup or BBQ sauce

1/4 cup caramelized onions
(optional)

NOTES:

WAFFLE-WICHES

Everyone loves waffles, and they are so easy to make - pop them in the toaster and you are good to go! But if you have only had them topped with syrup or whipped cream, then you are ignoring their multitude of uses.

All you need are some frozen microwaveable waffles, assorted sandwich fillings and some help from your kids. Once again, this is your chance to introduce kids to different flavors. Smoked salmon, hazelnut spread, different cheeses...whatever you like or your kids think looks interesting is something to try! Pairing new ingredients with a familiar food like waffles makes them less intimidating to kids and more likely that they will try and enjoy them!

FILLING IDEAS INCLUDE:

Scrambled Eggs and Salsa

Melted Munster Cheese and Jelly

Melted Cheddar Cheese and Apples

Bacon and Peanut or Almond Butter

Nutella and Fruit Slices

Cream Cheese and Smoked Salmon, Tomatoes, Onions

NOTES:

There is nothing like potatoes in the morning - filling, hearty and universally appealing. Feel free to add any veggies your kids like. Tater tots, crispy on the outside, creamy on the inside, meld with sausage, eggs and cheese to make a hearty, warming casserole that will make any kid forget about ketchup(though, truth be told, I love this with ketchup). Using chicken sausage makes this not only healthy, but also kosher!

DIRECTIONS

1} Preheat oven to 350° F

2} Layer tots in bottom of greased baking dish

3} Mix the rest of the ingredients in a bowl and pour over the tots

4} Bake for 45 minutes or until a knife put in the center of the casserole comes out clean

INGREDIENTS

1 32oz package Tater Tots

10 Eggs

1/2 cup Milk

1 lb Frozen pre-cooked Chicken Sausage
(links or patties, cut into bite size pieces)

1.5 cups Pepper Jack
(or whatever else you have lying around)

2 tsp. Salt

1 tbls. Pepper

Optional: chopped onions, bell peppers, tomatoes, mushrooms, etc.

NOTES:

BANANAS BRULEE

Incredibly easy and tastes more sinful than it really is. Just 2 ingredients give you a molten, crispy-melty mixture of creamy bananas and caramelized brown sugar.

DIRECTIONS

1} Line a baking sheet with tinfoil and set your oven to broil

2} Split the bananas with a knife lengthwise, and lay the banana boats, peel side down, on the baking sheet

3} Sprinkle the bananas evenly with the sugar

4} Place in the broiler for about 5 minutes, or until the sugar is bubbly and melted and the scent of caramel is wafting through your kitchen

INGREDIENTS

2 Bananas

1/4 cup Brown Sugar

NOTES:

APPLE GRANOLA STACKS

This is one of the healthiest breakfasts out there, and so delicious that your kids won't even know you are giving them something that's good for them. It's so delicious, you might even forget you are being healthy yourself!

DIRECTIONS

1} Core apple with apple corer if you have one (if not, skip to next step)

2} Cut each apple into 4 round slices, cutting across the apple width wise, not lengthwise. If you have not already cored the apple, cut the core out now, so you have 4 doughnut shaped slices per apple

3} Spread peanut butter on 4 of the 8 slices

4} Sprinkle granola and dried fruit on the peanut buttered slices

5} Top with the remaining apple slices and enjoy your small apple sandwiches

INGREDIENTS

2 Apples
(sweet ones, like Fuji or Gala work well here)

4 Tbs. Peanut Butter
(crunchy or creamy works well)

2 Tbs. Granola
(your favorite variety)

Small handful of raisins, dried cranberries, or other small dried fruit

NOTES:

BREAKFAST
NACHOS

If your kids have never had Mexican food, this is the chance to introduce them to the spice, flavor and nuances of this fantastic cuisine! They may not be ready for moles or tamales yet, but this super easy morning version of nachos is crunchy, creamy, zesty and filling. It brings together scrambled eggs, fragrant cilantro and crispy tortilla chips in a nacho dish that will have all your kids yelling "Arriba, Arriba!"

DIRECTIONS

1} Prepare Scrambled Eggs, including the 2 tsp of cumin. Remove, cover the pan to keep them warm and reserve for later

2} Arrange chips on a plate in an even layer

3} Dollop the beans and eggs on chips in an even layer

4} Add the cheese to the chips and microwave the dish for 30 seconds at a time until chips are hot and cheese is melted

5} Top with sour cream, cilantro, salsa and any other additional toppings, and enjoy

NOTES:

INGREDIENTS

1/2 Bag Tortilla Chips
(or however many your kids will eat. I prefer unsalted so you can control the spice level)

4 Scrambled Eggs and Onions
(from recipe above)
1/2 Cup Salsa

1 Cup Shredded Cheese
(preferably cheddar or pepper Jack, but literally, anything you have in the house will work.)

1 bunch cleaned cilantro (take the leaves off the stems and put the leaves in a deep bowl of cold water. Move the leaves around a bit with your hands then leave the leaves to soak and check the bowl in about 5 minutes. The dirt should all have fallen to the bottom of the bowl and the leaves should have floated to the top. Take out the leaves with your hands and dry them with a paper towel)

1 Can Refried Beans

1/3 Cup Sour Cream

2 tsp. Cumin

Optional Garnishes: Diced Avocado, Black Olives, Shredded Lettuce, Sliced Scallions, Leftover Taco or Hamburger Meat

BREAKFAST
PIZZA

Everyone loves pizza, and making it for breakfast is one way to get your kids into the kitchen and to get some vegetables into their day. There is no end to the variety of garden greens that kids will eat if it comes on a square of crispy pizza crust. This pizza uses store bought crust and sauce, a soft egg and a flurry of Parmesan cheese to entice even the pickiest eaters to a morning pizza party!

DIRECTIONS

1} Preheat oven as according to the directions on the pizza crust

2} Unroll pizza crust onto tin-foiled baking sheet

3} Spread sauce on crust

4} Crack each egg on a quarter of the pizza, keeping yolks intact

5} Put vegetables on the pizza, taking care not to disturb the egg yolks

6} Put pizza for as long as the directions say to let the crust cook – longer if the eggs are not yet set – still runny, but with whites fully firm. For the final 30 seconds or so of cooking, add the Parmesan cheese

7} When the cheese is browned, take out the pizza and serve

INGREDIENTS

1 Can Refrigerated Pizza Dough

4 Eggs

1 1/4 cups Tomato or Pesto sauce
(or a combination of the two)

1 cup Parmesan cheese

Assorted vegetables which may include but are not limited to: tomato, bell pepper, sliced red or yellow onion, black olive rings, jarred artichoke hearts, etc...

NOTES:

CHEESE & HAM BISCUITS

Try to find something easier than this, and you will be disappointed. If you think your kids might be into spicy foods, try topping it with some cayenne pepper – the combination of the salty ham, the creamy cheese and the spicy pepper is something that could awaken the chili-head in your kid.

DIRECTIONS

1} Preheat oven as directed on the biscuit package

2} Mix the cream cheese, cheddar cheese and ham together to make a paste

3} Remove biscuits from package

4} Split the biscuits open and put them on a tin-foiled baking sheet

5} Spread each one with an equal amount of cheese and ham , the cover the biscuit with its top and seal the edges so the inner cream cheese is totally concealed

6} Top each biscuit with a sprinkling of cayenne, if desired

7} Bake according to package directions and then enjoy

INGREDIENTS

1 Tube Refrigerated Biscuits
4 slices Deli Ham, diced into small pieces

1/2 cup Shredded Cheddar Cheese (plus more if needed)

1/2 cup Cream Cheese (any fat content will work)

1 tablespoon Cayenne pepper (optional)

NOTES:

SALMON SALAD SANDWICHES

Not every kid likes the taste of smoked salmon, but almost all of them love tuna sandwiches! This combination of a classic bagel and lox with a tuna sandwich will impress your kids and yourself. Switch out tuna for heart healthy canned salmon to make a breakfast sandwich that is so delicious you might find yourself having it for lunch and dinner, too!

DIRECTIONS

1} Mix the warm water, 1 tsp. at a time, into the cream cheese until the cream cheese is slightly loose, but still very thick, like the consistency of mayonnaise. You may not use all the water – the point here is to loosen up the cream cheese so you can mix it with the salmon without breaking up the salmon flakes

2} Fold the salmon flakes, onion, salt and pepper into the cream cheese with a spoon, being careful not to break up the salmon too much

3} Spread the salmon mixture on half of the toasted bagel, and top with cucumber and tomato, and serve

INGREDIENTS

2 Toasted Bagels, split

6 oz. can of Salmon, drained and flaked

4 oz. Cream Cheese, softened

2 tbls. Warm Water, plus more if needed

1/4 Red Onion, minced

4 slices Cucumber

2 slices Tomato

1 tsp Salt

2 tsp Pepper

NOTES:

GRILLED FRUIT W/ NUTELLA, COTTAGE CHEESE & YOGURT DIP

This is so simple it doesn't even need a recipe.

DIRECTIONS

1} You just cut up fruit – any fruit – bananas, pineapple, plums, peaches – and throw them on the grill or under the broiler for 3-4 minutes or until the fruit smells sweet and starts to turn deep brown along the edges

2} Then, serve it alongside Nutella (hazelnut chocolate spread), low fat vanilla yogurt and cottage cheese mixed with honey for an elegant and fun fondue breakfast

NOTES:

BREAKFAST FOR DESSERT FOR BREAKFAST

This is a very sweet breakfast and might be best as a treat instead of an everyday occurrence, but the look of the plate will delight your kids and the ease of making it will delight you.

DIRECTIONS

1} Take the Nutella and dollop it onto a piece of greased cling wrap (VERY lightly greased with butter, vegetable oil or spray)

2} Wrap the Nutella up loosely in the wrap, then roll the wrap on a hard surface until it makes a cylinder

3} Put the Nutella log in the fridge to firm

4} Drain peaches and throw away the juice/syrup in which they were canned

5} Divide the marshmallow fluff onto two plates and make them into a perfect circle, either freeform or using a cookie cutter or other mold

6} Place 1 peach into the center of each plate of your fluff – this is the egg yolk

7} Heat the jam in the microwave for 5 seconds at a time until it is runny, then drizzle it over the "eggs" to make your "hot sauce"

8} Remove the Nutella from the fridge, unwrap it, and cut it into 4 equal pieces. These are your sliced "sausages"

9} Serve alone or with slices of pound cake or angel food cake

INGREDIENTS

1 can of halved Peaches
(or 4 peach halves)

1/2 cup Marshmallow Fluff

1/2 cup Nutella

2 tsp. Red Jam or Jelly
(raspberry, strawberry, mixed berry, etc.)

2 slices of Pound or Angel Food Cake (optional)

NOTES:

APPLE BUTTER ALMOND S'MORES

Marshmallows and chocolate aren't the only ways to enjoy a campfire favorite! This microwave version uses heart healthy almonds, zippy cinnamon and juicy apples to create a breakfast so delicious your kids will think it's dessert!

DIRECTIONS

- Mix the cinnamon and the almond butter in a bowl until blended

- Spread the almond butter mixture evenly on the graham crackers

- Microwave the graham crackers for 10 seconds at a time, until almond butter is warm and looks slightly runny

- Layer apples on the graham crackers and close the crackers up to make sandwiches

INGREDIENTS

4 Whole Graham Crackers

4 Tbls. Almond Butter
(room temperature)

1 Apple, sliced

2 Tsp. Cinnamon

NOTES:

ABOUT THE AUTHOR:

Sarah Spigelman is a writer, editor and food lover from birth. Her writing has been featured on The Huffington Post, The Daily Meal and many nationally distributed magazines. She lives in NYC, where she splits her time between seeing Broadway shows and eating food so spicy that it makes her nose run. She chronicles her NYC eating adventures on her personal website www.fritosandfoiegras. com and blogs about food for the food site of Today Show.

Made in the USA
Middletown, DE
11 December 2018

Super Emotions!

A Book for Bipolar Children

by Lionel Lowry IV

To Lillie, Laander, Leah, my parents, Tim, and all of my family, and friends along the way,

Keep laughing - *Lionel*

Super Emotions!
A Book for Bipolar Children

by

Lionel Lowry IV

This book belongs to ...

_____

Breathe in.

Breathe out.

Relax.

Good morning.

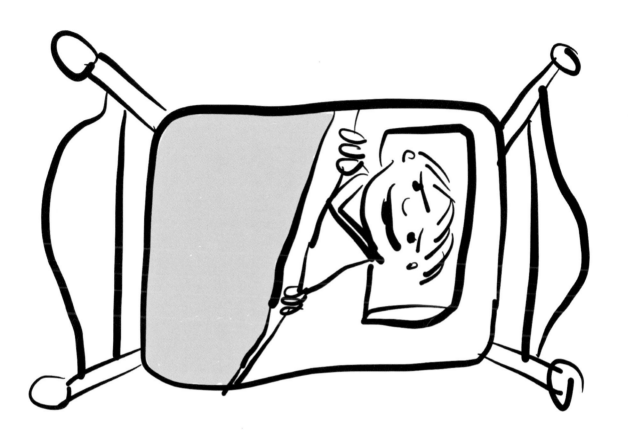

So they say you are bipolar,

So what does this mean, my friend?

This means you have Super Emotions,

And you need to learn to control them.

Your emotions give you power,

Power to dream and think, and play.

Learn to use them correctly,

And you'll be A-Okay.

When you are happy, you may be very, very happy,

When you are sad, you may be oh so very sad,

When you are excited, you may be extremely excited,

And when you are angry, you may be incredibly MAD!

Your parents and your doctors

Will help show you what to do.

They will ask lots of questions and give you tests,

They will work hard to help you.

Sometimes you will feel so happy,

You'll want to jump and scream, and shout.

Make sure that it's appropriate where you are,

You don't want to get thrown out.

Sometimes you will feel so sad,

Like everything is bleak and bad.

Just remember how much your family loves you,

Good feelings will come back, and you'll feel great and glad.

There are many things you can try,

When your feelings get to you.

Two of them are exercise and art,

Try them and they will help you through.

Paint, draw, dance,

Run, skip, and swim,

Let your Super Emotions flow,

And you will start to feel better again.

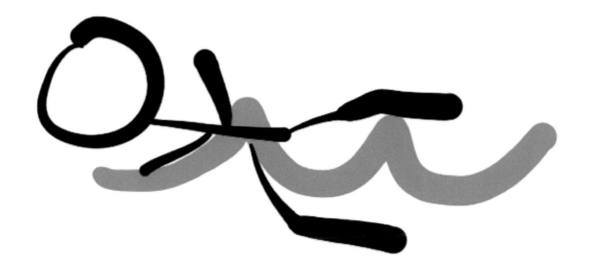

You have the Super Powers,

To help your Super Self calm down.

Believe in yourself and try every day,

You are a Super Hero, be proud!

Super Hero, you are loved,

Every part of you is fantastic.

Your Super Emotions make you special,

Just help them be less drastic.

It's time to rest your Super Emotions,

And let peace fill your soul.

Let yourself be calm and relaxed,

And let your Super Self take control.

Breathe in.

Breathe out.

Relax.

Good night.

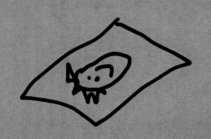

shhhh... the end

Friends,

If you like this Super Emotions! book, and think it might help others, please ask them to visit www.SuperEmotions.com

We are a group of youth-minded people dedicated to enriching lives and empowering children. We appreciate your support.

Thank you!

Sincerely,

Lionel

Made in the USA
Las Vegas, NV
04 January 2021